Conchas y Café Zine
Vol. VIII, Issue 1

See My Words

a  publication

DSTL Arts presents

See My Words

Conchas y Café Zine
Vol. VIII, Issue 1

Cover and Book Design: Luis Antonio Pichardo

ISBN: 978-1-946081-64-3

10 9 8 7 6 5 4 3 2 1

www.DSTLArts.org

Los Angeles, CA

Contents

Why Poetry?

Luz Donis

Because
there is

an impenetrable
insurmountable
wall of Metaphor
which only poets have
to chip away

Because
of a mind

too narrow
and infinite
dots to connect

Because
We are running

out of time
to change
our idea
of the world

Because
You need to
exhaust
all the words

find

the silence

and
believe again

The Process of Joy

Stephanie Paola Salas

Sensitive and slow,
I listen

to each sound
caress my ears,

each consonant
brush my lips,

each emphasis
echo in my own pulse.

No one is here
to say
delicada.

Here, I fit, for now.
Intentional

with every decision,
every line

break.

I can't rush this
love.

POET W O R D S

Dr. Rosie Ramos

POET W O R D S are unique.
I love pouring out
My feelings and emotions
On aesthetically metamorphosed tree products.
Your thoughts and emotions are intriguing to this Poet
The conscious mind; the iceberg above sea level, navigates a
Poet's pen
To create unless *W O R D S.*
My imagination and *W O R D S* freely travel
Like Pegasus;
The symbol of freedom and creative inspiration!
Dare to catch those *W O R D S*
That appeal to you, yet some WORDS may slip by and mean nothing.
I merely ask
Hear me out!
My *W O R D S* will climb
Onto conscious minds; like magical river streams of life dreams
For the believers.
Imagine the iceberg that steers and controls the course your
conscious mind
Drifts slowly above your sea's surface mind, craving to be challenged
by others.
You see my *W O R D S*
You feel my *W O R D S*
Zealous to expand your conscious iceberg
With this Poet's unique *W O R D S.*

Mírame a mi

Sanjuanita Martinez

¿Otra vez, tu soñando?
Pero que no ves que fácil es
Tomar la pluma y un papel
¿Y plasmar tus letras en él?
Si dejaras de soñar,
Tal vez ya tendrías tu primer ejemplar.
Mírame a mí, hasta premios ya gané.
El Premio Nacional fue el primero en llegar.

Y es que esperas y esperas
Pensando que no lo mereces
Porque crees que tus letras
Puedan sonar algo rebeldes.

Escribe lo que te apasiona.
El pasado, presente o futuro,
Del bello recuerdo de tu infancia
O aquel momento tan oscuro.

Escribe de lo mágico del sol
O del beso tan añorado
Del esplendor de la luna
O tal vez del silencio
En un día tan apurado.

Musas no hay, no lo olvides.
Mejor toma tu papel de raya.
Enciende la radio y déjate ir.
Pon a Blades, Bublé o Santana
Que el tiempo es oro se dice.
Y no sabemos si hay mañana.

Breath of Life

Lois Jackson King

Creatively given, it was never yours to keep
He can extend it, but it is His to reclaim

Will not last forever; so use it well
In this vast world of diversities
Before time will know you no more

Breathe, breathe, the breath, out
Don't dare hold it back

Breathe out, Spirit of Truths
And that which enhances one's life
Allow that breath to burst out

Let it come forth, as a mighty wind
Ash to ashes and dust to dust

Flesh dies, the spirit shall never die
Forever forward, a legacy to leave
Received by welcome ears the breath from the All Mighty
The breath that gave life

Breathe it out to help each other
Encourage one another
A spiritual journey worthwhile

The mind, the heart to the "Pen"
Leave a trail, leading to

A strong sense of resilience

Never to give way to negativity
Then your living will not be in vain

Profanity

Michelle Smith

Can you cuss like a sailor?
Are your words sharp as a razor?
And do they sting like a bee
Or a gun of a taser?

Profanity,
A well-done,
Thickly layered sandwich popping like
Flaming Hot Cheetos in your mouth.

Full of flavor,
Maybe unwavered,
And a habit I savored.

Profanity,
Profanity,
Excessive
Or
Expressive,
But
Full
Of
Labor.

Writing Prompts

Alayna Abravanel

What I did over the weekend is I got my flu shot on Wednesday evening, and I was so brave I did not cry or move; and basically it is because I sat still. I screamed a little bit, but after that I went to the library. Before I get my flu shot and reading books and having a class online on Zoom and tutoring to help me, it makes me feel better, and rowing makes me smarter and smarter, and my goal is to get a job working at Starbucks and becoming a barista and customer service.

What do you think the job is related to? Do you get along with people and you shake hands when the interviewer says the job? Well, my main goal is to become professional and not gossip with other people and be rude, or make mean faces just to get mad. How should this person handle this situation, and what happens if a stranger is bullying you, do you scream or do you walk away?

Almost a Coffee Haiku

Michelle Smith

Bubbles on my saucer
and a cup of Joe.
Clouds in my coffee,
the scent of steam
flows through an open window.

Apoco si

Captain Chale (aka Abraham Jaramillo)

Apoco si...
I, break the silence
after all, this person has talked
for more than 30 minutes, and
due to my sitting I couldn't walk
out, I wish I had put a sock in his mouth

Chale, chale, chale... me vas a decir
you did all this,
set up a successful business,
selling this and that,
who knows what,
yet you want to help us,
did I miss anything,
or does this sounds like
a *pinche* pyramid scheme

"Sr. I just want to help my
community, make them
and you, financially successful,"
the presenter energetically said
pointing, *con un anillote en cada dedo*,
then I said,
señor, yo no me chupo el dedo,
and yet I didn't pull the trigger
on my middle finger,
yet

Aver, aver, aver...
you haven't shown us the
number of sales and profits, and

you barely said anything, *acerca*
de este grandioso producto,
ah pero eso si,
you have, in detail,
shown us how to get more,
team members... that should report
to us,
who in return report to someone,
who then, I assume, will report
to you,

I turn to the crowd,

The presenter... is a scammer, not your savior,
Then I pull the trigger and walk out.

Two Faces

Lois Jackson King

What is it you are saying
Have you been cut in two
Are there two of you

One day you are so sweet
Just like a piece of candy
The next day, dry and sandy

What with the switch-a-roo
What has gotten a hold of you
The better you seems depressed

A true bitterness causing you stress
You are now stirring up a mess
Eager to be mean than be nice

I'm not judging; just my observation
From a distance, afar
I really don't know who you are

Just making notes of what I see
In hopes evil forces will set you free
a great change in you will be

For who can say about tomorrow
The sweeter you just might follow
Does anything ever stay the same

Will it bring more meanness and sorrow
It's pushing you to an uncontrolled end

The evilness hurt family and friends

Tell me where will it all end

Educated Fool

Royal Roots

Educated fool,
No amount of years in school
Can ever teach you what I do.

This wisdom cannot be taught,
Much less, by a man,
Who could never understand.

Respect the women
From which humanity came.
We birthed the nations.
We nurtured the world.

How dare YOU TELL ME,
I'm doing it wrong!

We've been birthing this way all along.
Until you came with your
control and ways to make money.
Suppress my powers
With your pharmaceuticals.

I refuse all your wizardry.
I'll stand in my ancestral ways.
Your scientists are still
Catching up
To the wisdom embedded in me.

Consider The Source

Lois Jackson King

Consider the whole matter
Are "U" just some mad hater
Help change things from the latter

Consider

Not just for "U"
Not just for "Me"
Not just for "Them"

Consider

Together, we should stand
Let's make it our future plan
Moving forward hand in hand

Consider

Not being a bumbler
Not even a crumblier
"VOTE"; it hurt from tumblers

Consider

Standing for something
Don't just accept just anything
"WE" count, aim for the gold ring

Consider

Standing together making a choice
Lift up loud, everyone, our voice
No more being quiet, let's a big noise

Yo

Sanjuanita Martinez

Do not slam the door!
Put the seat down!
Correct with love!
Trash!
This is me, again.

Chingao!
¡Ay no, otra vez!
¿Dónde puse las llaves?
¿Loca yo?
¡Gorda, que gorda estoy!
Oh well, it has set in with time.
I laugh out loud.
This is me, again.

"I am late again,"
Did not mean to.
I always wait for you!
No, you don't.
I wait for you.
Again, this is me.

Fakata!
¡No apagué la estufa!
Se me olvidó mi bolsa.
Bitchy attitude, like always.
What did you say?
I thought you didn't cuss.
I did not!
Fakata!
¡Otra vez yo!

Clouds of Cotton On My Mouth

Abraham Jaramillo

The worst nightmare
Open   your mouth
dental   affair

All   worries   banished
the miracle   of
modern   healthcare

My   tongue
cares   not
of   words
so soft   everything
my fingers   touch

I   glide   on
the back   seat
of   my   ride   home

Clouds   of   fivers
on   my   mouth
my   driver's   mission
done   I   am
Home.

My Bones Are Worthless

Dr. Rosie Ramos

Oh NO!

My

torn

rotator

cuff

  pieces

of bones

        still connected

     to this

       crooked

    body   drags me down
                  like an old rusty
                 dangling heavy chain.

                 Ugh! Had to stop swimming,
                 dancing and exercising!

               "Poor genes,
                  bone deterioration,
            your age,"
                 My doctor said.

                 Iyiyi!...OUCH!
                   Surgery needed!!!!

       I've cried and prayed...what else is left?

             "Try imagery, music,
              a glass of wine
             to calm down,"

My Nutritionist said.

"Hey, forget the wine and booze it up...!"
My Amigos said.

So the hell in tormenting

    myself of my future pain,

        I'm gonna LIVE it up with................**MY** *sabrosa Tequila Tequila*

That's Real

Lois Jackson King

Heart attack had no gain
I made it, without a lot of pain
I feel like going on
That's real
Many illnesses had a claim
Who holds the blame
I feel like standing strong
That's real
Pain forcing me to yell out
Even into a mighty shout
I feel like life is not long
That's real
Cancer made an entry
A life full of worry
I feel like going on
That's real
As you can plainly see
From cancer I am free
I feel like singing a song
That's real
Not focusing on the past
Looking toward the future at last
I feel like enjoying a new way of life
That's real

Vintage Tigress

Michelle Smith

"I'm not a spring chicken, I'm a wise hen."
–Michelle Y. Smith

I've got homework to do
for my poetry class. Let's go
Chris and set the table for
El Pollo Loco before 6:30
tonight.

And again our family
friend and caregiver's
tardiness has
no bounds, for he is not
around.

Excuse me and
what's your problem?
Peace and quiet
are important and
so is timeliness for Chris,
Bozo the Clown!

My Tuesday and Wednesday
class is my self-care.
Knowledge is power.

Communication is my jewel
and for my classmates
I craft with radiance and sparkle.

We take turns and
think about what to write.

I am the Vintage Tigress
on the poetry and prose prowl.
I'm known as Ms. Michelle,
and never a senior student.
You've got that right!

Enjambment and stanzas
and their importance is what
our Maestro plans to tell.

Draft after draft I will not
be forlorn. Don't tear up my
piece of paper from
a seething page that has
my hot ink and blazing
words scorned.

Tuesday and Wednesday
is my poetry class
a.k.a. Conchas y Cafe.

Where's my pan dulce
and champurrado
to quell my hunger for the next
hour and a half
and the August
into November days, nights,
and tomorrow?

Remember You Were Young

Lois Jackson King

We all are apt to error
Don't be so hard-minded
Many environments are different
Good morning, eat your breakfast
Have a nice day at school
A peaceful spirit for the day
When we were young
Did we listen all the time
We wanted our distance
Time has made a difference
What is said most today
Eat at school
I'll be working late
TV dinner in fridge
They jerked out the door
Apt to shy away or be a bully for the day
I tell you here and now
Watch how you interact
Each child is an individual
So please encourage their strengths
Uplift and equip their young minds
Help our children to be champions

The Invisible Woman

Luz Donis

Now you see me
Now you don't

You don't really
                              get me
No longer want you
                              to try
Move over, just let me
                                        walk on by

Now you see me
Now you don't

I don't owe you a thing
I harness energy
                              converge
to a being
                              Mi Nagual
something of which
you   know   nothing

Now you see me
Now you don't

You've forgotten my past
          I have, just as fast
A giant eraser
wiped clean
                              that slate
I defied death
you never knew

my fate

The Valley Girl Conundrum

Stephanie Paola Salas

Okay, so, yeah.
Maybe I do,
you know,
talk like a

"valley girl."

Honestly, I don't even try, like,
it just comes out.
I can't help that
the valley is

my birthright.

San Fernando?
I don't really know
who that is, but I'm sure he's cool…
Closer to the coast, right?

Closer than this dry basin,

that nobody really knows,
but that I know
like I know the wrinkles
on my palms.

This "Central" Valley,

I guess, is home?
I feel like,

when I'm home,
all of me should be accepted.

When I'm home, I'll know it.

Yet, this valley,
that's supposed to be my valley,
hasn't seemed to take me in
the way I've taken in

the verdant fields,
the grumpy cows,
the VOCs blowing in the wind.
Yes, I talk like where I come from,

but I can't, like, totally be myself.

I can't say,
"Dang, girl, okay"
and "utterly impressive"
in the same context.

Why? God, you put me here,

with a purpose and a passion,
and a love for people,
but Mighty Jesus,
where do I belong?

A Crowd

Lois Jackson King

A crowd can be overpowering,
like a road of heavy traffic in your space
Many times, a crowd can place you in fearful situations
making life scary, moving us, in haste
The next thing you know,
like in my life, you have a case,
strangers are all up in your face
Other times, a crowd has made a change
in character, of how a person lives; there for all to see
When they say, will you please
using this phrase, I tell them, stop breathing all over me
Like all crowds, they have their way
to persuade a direction,
never by you was its intention
Just like undesired traffic
by your side, drivers with silent looks
power to make you cry
Crowds have power
sending people like me to a place
where I haven't been before
The pushy, mind-blowing crowd
can be called a strong herd
and can initiate the wrong door.
This crowd of people,
you and I, may hang out with for a time
at environmental events
Continually pushing us forcefully
toward a style of life they themselves did invent
When the power of this crowd
is pushing in a direction we have not planned
I have learned to stop all the foolishness
and have a chat with my inner man

I decided to take a new path
and entrust my direction into God's hand
I am as strong as I want to be
and I am able to live
and achieve without a crowd
All I need
God has already placed in me;
and in my sense of self, I must be proud
you are free, to decide the same,
then you will surely understand
the crowd is not in command
A loving fellowship
in God's love has always been His plan.

Alter Ego (My Alternate Self)

Nameless Soul (aka Dr. Rosie Ramos)

Who struggles through
my protective shield,
nameless soul, flat-affect, yet
dependent, timeless,

yet unrevealed; whose lively
motions can be concealed?

Intermittently I heard
inner roars as "friends" from the past
encouraged street drugs and fighting,
like unwavering, punishing, relentless,

swarm of hornets surrounding this teen girl
who lived amongst them;
the inner roars proceed to breakthrough,
becoming transcendent. Succumbing to this teen

outburst emotions—a larger-than-life strong human
Nameless Soul, when pissed, transforms to a dependable,
brilliantly–intense red/green color. Enraged,
one powerful punch deforms

entire corrupt cities and her Rottweiler devouring "friends"
with superpowers when needed,
are performed and when done,
the red/green colors subside and gentle

submission of calmness
is felt. This one, I know

you know, makes me
feel strong, protected; comes between
the natural growing
bones and muscles, from mind and heart,

especially when growing up,
rage kept this teen girl apart.
Family's love built her integrity
and moral values, the Almighty's best piece of art.

I still have reasons for my **Nameless Soul** to hang
around longer, now as the adult. You know me best,
my thoughts and feelings
when happy or not.

Mom's Self Talk

Royal Roots

The sunshine beams through the window.
Thank Creator,
Another day,
Time to get up and start adulting.

Aaahhhh…
The baby screams for the *chi chi*.
Grateful to God my body is the nourishment she needs.
Oh good, she's done,
And stayed asleep.

Better get up
Cuz once they wake up,
There's no free time.
No me time.
It's one thing after another.

Time to clean time.
The tub needs a good scrub…
The sink looks a mess.
Oh, gosh… look at those rings on the toilet.
And that's just the bathroom.
I dread inspecting the rest of the house.

Ok… Ok… Focus,
One thing at a time.
The restroom first,
Then we can see if there's time
For anything else.

Wish it would stay this clean,
But I'll be realistic.
As soon as they wake up,
Breakfast crumbs will fly all over.

Ugh… oh well,
I still gotta do it;
I am the only adult.

Great job, mom,
You finished the bathroom
Now to sweep up.

I hear some noise from the room,
A high pitch, "good morning, mami," follows.

Creator give me strength the day
Is about to really go.
But I know time flies and
I remind myself I am blessed.
And if Creation takes care of
All the animals and plants,
I got this.

"Grand rising, darling.
Go brush your teeth."
I peek in the room,
One down,
two to go.

I let them sleep in
While I finish breakfast.
Food always gets my boy.
He comes in like Pepe Le Pieu.
"What's for breakfast, mom?"

Never fails.

Constantly reminding them
"Be quiet,
The baby
Is sleeping."

Now I understand the phrase
My daddy used to say,
"Goes in one ear,
And out the other."

I wonder when I became my parents,
But I hear them a lot.

"Time to eeeeaaatttt."
I wonder if they did a good job
Brushing their teeth.

"What are we eatinnggg?"
"Food." I respond.
"And let's be grateful
We have food."
… that's definitely my dad talking.

"–but I don't like…"
Ugh, here we go.
Ok, relax, you used to be an ungrateful, picky eater when you
            were their age,
Try to understand them.

"Well, guys we don't always eat what we like,
We have to learn to eat different foods."
"–but we don't like vegetables."
"Well, hunny we're vegetarian,

That's what we eat."

You'd think they're part French
By the time they take to eat.

Ok. School time.
But they stay home
And I school them.

Sometimes I wonder what I got myself into.
But not just home-school,
Motherhood in general.
No manual, no instructions... nothing...

Reading time is always welcomed.
Well, at least the picture books.

Bathroom time is never private,
Not in a house with toddlers.
I tell them the door slightly open
Is NOT an invitation,
But to hear they're ok.

But, sometimes, baby's still with me.
Yup, breastfeeding... Attached to the boob...
Me on the toilet.
Hey, when ya gotta go, ya got to go
Oh... the horrors of being a mom.

I gotta get it together,
Time to go outside,
Maybe a bike ride,

I need to get a little high.
A little hit to get mom

Back in the mood to deal
With all these moods.

Each child different.
It's a rollercoaster most days.
And trying to keep my cool,
I need some hierbitas.

Stigma, eh, who needs your judgment?
Your shit stinks too.
I do what I got to do,
To survive and push myself to strive.

I think herb is medicine.
But eh... back to real life,
And now it's writing time.

They need help, a little reminder to slow down,
Take their time, it's all right...
Whew, thank God for ganjah
My patience was reloaded.

Break time, snack time, frutitas to the rescue,
With vitaminas and hydration.
... way better mood than candy cuz of aspartame.
Yay, mom, helping them choose better.

Ok, time for art... with the baby on the boob.
"Both of your art is beautiful in its own way.
Stop being mean to one another,
That's not why you have a sister or a brother."

Is it time for dad to come home yet?
Man, I neeeed a break,
Even a trip to the store for tortillas.

Snap, I gotta get dinner started.
But let me feed the baby again...

Frijolitos nunca faltan.
How many ways I can cook em,
I never counted,
But how I've grown to love this ancient food.
Today, no one will complain;
Bean pupusas with curtido y salsa,
Is always a treat.
Two salsas; one with lots of chiles, none in the other.

"Papi," they all yell.
Even the baby shrieks for dad.
It is total bliss to witness this.
I love the way they love him,
And the way he loves them.

He looks so tired,
But they sparkle his eyes right up.
I'm grateful I have food ready for him.
He gets paid to build the city,
I stay home and get kisses and hugs
To be a mom, a nurse, a teacher, a preacher, a friend, a cook, a
        motivational speaker, a cleaner, and any
Other role needed.

We all sit and enjoy this ancestral food.
I remind my children that due to this ancestral food,
Maize and frijol,
We are still here and we are still strong.

Then we get ready for danza.
Another way we are learning to reconnect with the ancient ways
        we did things.

Sometimes my children like it, sometimes they don't.
It always fills me, and I try to go every chance I get.
Smelling the ceremony smoke and listening to the drums fills
my soul.

I feel so light on the way home.
Here comes another battle.
To put them all to sleep,
Oh, child that can be a challenge.
A back and forth.
They get thirsty, they gotta go pee and then they wanna talk
about the books we read.

Ugh, another bowl sounds calming.
It just started getting quiet.
A little sativa to stimulate my artistic side.
What will it be tonight?
Crochet... drawing...
Sewing... no, too loud.
I just fed the baby and she fell asleep.
Maybe painting or writing poetry?

Not tonight,
Exhaustion carried me away mid-plan.

"Happy Man, Happy Wife," Or So They Say

Sanjuanita Martinez

There lived a very happy man
With a very unhappy wife
Who hoped and hoped
Every now and then
For a very different life.

Dirty floors, dirty dishes, laundry galore.
Gazillion toys all strewn on the floor.
Children crying, screaming, fighting.
Uncooked meals awaiting on the stove.
Was that an old phone ringing off the wall?
And the hubby… with the bros?

"But woman," he would say.
"You just complain and complain
because that's all you do all day."
Grow up! Tackle life like I do.
Be happy like me.
I do not worry at all
About life's affairs.
I just work and play.

"But husband of mine," she muttered,
"How right you are!"
I know little about life.
For all I do is sit and count the little I have.
I failed to learn the ABCs or the 123s
Of life.
As you say, I do nothing all day

Just complain, complain, and complain.

Now go on and be happy.
Your dinner will not be served.

"Woo" The Future

Lois Jackson King

Oh the toils of times with decisions to make
Why has talking back and rebellion
become the trend of today
Our youth are encompassed by social warfare
by controlling what they do and say
If we don't try and help
they will soon have to pay
The educated and fancy words are spoken
but so much knowledge they need to seek
they are trying to be strong and not weak
Trends and styles dictate the
"it's all about money in the bank"
seeking to belong, and all day long they're on the phone
Knowing not what to seek out, or their future to protect
Who will help them to achieve, who can help in what to believe
Let us set an example, the best we can
This one way to lend a helping hand
Many of them have more experience than we
But so misguided like fallen fruit from a tree
Let them know that they matter too
No more or no less, just as important as me and you

Awesome and Anew

Michelle Smith

A Palos Verdes branch stuck me
on the back of my hand.
A prick with no blood.
An ouch of pain.
It was "a touch it and you'll get burned"
kind of thing.
Seedlings each with three colors,
wispy on the ground.
They are shedding onto
the gray concrete of
Benny Potter Park:
yellow floral sprigs
kissed with a cinnamon
red hot candy center
nestled green needle branches.
The Ides of March and sky wind were dancing.
How Awesome and Anew.

The Cempoaxochil

Royal Roots

Life is
evanescent.

We bloom,
Then wither,

As rapidly
as the
Cempoaxochil.

Búsquenme y allí estaré

Sanjuanita Martinez

Desde el cantar de algún colorido jilguero
En el verdor de la primavera
Búsquenme en la sombra de un buen árbol
Mientras a lo lejos vendrá un recuerdo mío.
Sabrán que aún les cuido.

Desde el desasosegar de las olas
En ese verano que se ha asomado,
Déjense consentir por las gaviotas
Y al regocijarse en su canto al viento,
Escucharán musitar mis palabras en el mar.

Desde el remolinear de las hojas
En el triste otoño
Atiendan el silencio
Hasta que ensordezca
Y al percibir mis suspiros
Sentirán que aún les acompaño.

Desde el caer de las frías gotas
En el congelado invierno
Respiren hondo y tendido
Hasta que el aire puro lo sientan
Y respirarán al compás mío.

Búsquenme,
Cuando más quieran sentir mi esencia,
Cierren los ojos, suspiren, escuchen el silencio
Y poco a poco tranquilizarán sus almas.
Y allí estaré.

Food for the Spirit

Lois Jackson King

What are you speaking into your Spirit Man?
What are you downloading?
Who can help you when you call?

The Voice in you, which will not let you fall
Yes, to you and to you alone, your life is speaking
Your inner (Spirit Man) values and worth are, crying to be heard

Feed the Spirit, the stuff which will make you emotionally, and
    spiritually strong
The food pantry is in you; think first, about how you should start
From the right voice of spiritual nutrition, you must not depart

The best spiritual receipts are found in the Holy Book
Mindfully take the time; search the facts and give it a good look
You will find growth, in self-esteem, and other needs.

Don't be fooled, there are rules to fight by, guidelines for love.
Words of understanding, for business and managing the home
All you have to do is read the word for (Holy Bible) "Abundance
    of life"

Your life is in your hands. Hear the voice of your heart's plea.
With or without the voice of a book, your life is still, in your hands
    to form what you will be
Freedom to decide what to do. Inner man, speak; give directions.
    Help me to be strong

My inner voice is pushing me forth and forever forward;
My voice shall be heard loud and clear inward and outward.

My Tree

Michelle Smith

My tree to climb is the
ladder of life. Family branches in
all lengths. The roots that cement
my ancestry are from deep and rich
sepia soil and foundation.

Extensions and connections are
leaves of love. My parentage
is my father's sunlight and shade
protection from nature's elements.
My mother's lessons of color, crispness, clarity: her perseverance
        and strength.

With those seasons from youth to old,
my tree to climb is more valuable than
the autumn of red, brown, and gold.

I'll Take *THAT* Leap!

Dr. Rosie Ramos

I love to stride through the streets of East L.A.
La Virgin's mural comes to life and blesses me every day;
Speaking Spanish, English, Spanglish in the 70's—RAZA WE WON!
La Virgin's presence… then and today… makes me feel safe, you
       know! I'm okay.

Dolores' *"Si Se Puede"* words teaches us gente piel canela
Que Viva Hope! Viva la Pasión! Viva Courage! VIVA LA RAZA!
WE sacrificed, successfully marched, united, and protested **THEN**;
Today, it's complicated, you know! A ver que pasa.

Many changes made, yet many more must come.
Mi Gente! Never give up or become complacent; remember—
       where you from!
The past—Hung out with my carnales, a beer in hand, we rode in
       fancy ranflas on weekends
Down Whittier Boulevard while listening to 'Oldies But Goodies'
       rolas was the bomb!

Live with passion, commitment and cariño; y a la brava con todo.
Reach out to family, friends, especially the Almighty; but never
       ride solo.
It is what it is, you know! Don't allow yourself to become numb.
Hold your head up high and trust yourself because you are not
       just a so-so!

I made a promise to myself that I must keep.
Go For It—You Know! It's your life so don't be cheap;
My future path is uncertain—You Know! But I'll take *THAT* leap!
My future path is uncertain—You Know! **But I'll take *THAT* leap!**

BLACKNESS BLOOMS

Michelle Smith

*"The blacker the berry, the sweeter the juice." The bigger the
tree, the stronger the roots."*
—Wallace Henry Thurman and Tupac Shakur

My Blackness Blooms buds in all shades
as in petals of a rose.
I'm beautifully fragrant and sweet. Watch out for my thorns.

As in the museum, look, but don't touch,
yet you know you want to.
Admire me from afar. Harriet Tubman
taught the world about and from the
North Star.

My Blackness Blooms in a hummingbird.
Jeweled toned in rainbow colors.
Harmonious in feathered flight.
Tasting floral nectar. Small in stature.
Yet mighty and undisturbed. For a thing
of beauty is a joy forever.
Colonialism doesn't fly here; unity does.

My Blackness will grate on your nerves
and mind. Your envy. You're bewitched,
bewildered, and bothered. Your struggle is wanting the forbidden
          fruit and tempted
as Eve was in the Garden of Eden.

Your stalemate as thoughts and words
utter the N-word, yet cultural assimilation with full-lipped Botox,

cornrows, and box braids is cool.

The struggle is real as in the 1947 "Race Records" spun on the
old Victrola record player in a picket fence suburban house.
A jockey in the front yard. And like fine wine we fellowship and
mellow in
melanin and age.

My Blackness Blooms don't crack and
the world will not stop emulating.

Pretty Face, Sad Eyes

Royal Roots

Walking the slums
Of the city.
Only thing colder than the concrete streets
Are these city hearts,
Hardened by life's arduous struggles.

Suddenly...
I see the most beautiful girl I've ever seen.
Our eyes lock, souls connect,
Like sisters,
We feel the other's sadness.

Divine is her name,
She tells me.
But by the look on her face
I can see her life has been everything but;
From the tattoos that cover her angelic face
To the piece of clothes draped across her model shape.
Treated like a hard rock,
When she really is a gem.

She reaches over
And offers me the only thing she got;
Four cookies in an opened pack
And a goddess smile,
She just warmed my heart.

I smile back and I know,
She feels the sincerity.
I thank her,
Grateful for her existence.

She rushes across the street
As the street light flashes.
I say a silent prayer,
She probably did the same.

"Dear God,
 Please protect that girl in the hood,
 The one with a pretty face and sad eyes."

Celebration of My Voice That Will Not Be Quieted Down

Dr. Rosie Ramos

My FAMILIA—dysfunctional yet juntos como chicle!
Enmeshed, como mashed potatoes with no individualized
      self-identity
Dysfunctional, yelling and arguing for senseless reasons,
         As long as I got the last word in!
Yet we all realize the importance of
         Keeping this crazy family together by embracing family
         gatherings
         Although living miles away from each other with;
Cantos de amor y Cariño
         Guitarras, maracas, claves y tambores
         Singing Rancheras, Baladas and Oldies but Goodies;
Homemade aroma comidas
         Tamales, sopas, caldos y mas that even without a gust
         of wind,
         Smoothly fills the atmosphere, intrudes through our nostrils
         as we drive
         Closer from different directions to reach *La Casa*;
Muchas Fiestas
         Piñatas de lindos colores
         Y tequila for everyone!

My ANCESTORS—antique and recent fotos!
Chain of descendants
Welcoming your guidance
Constantly visit your Altar...
         Sarapes de muchos colores drape your table, calaveras,
         lit-up red, green, and white candles
         Melt onto the platitos, shining a flickering light from the
         candles onto each foto,

Of my brave ancestors who paved the ways of life
With their callous, cut-up, changed colors of aging hands
from hard labor
Combined with long hours of walking the picket line to
fight for equality;
Offering Gifts for your journeys beyond…
Supernatural inner strengths of confidence and a bold,
persuasive voice I gain from all of YOU!

Brimming

Stephanie Paola Salas

Heart overflows

onto my lap.

About the Authors
.... Sobre los autores

Luz Donis

A second-generation Guatemalan and second-generation L.A. County Nurse. Born in Chi-town raised in Boyle Heights. I've had the privilege of working, volunteering, and serving my community. It's been a joy finding my Spanish, English and Spanglish voice and expressing it through the *Conchas y Café Zine.*

Stephanie Paola Salas

Stephanie Paola has the hope of Christ in her soul, and she hopes her writing can reflect its healing power. Check out more of her writing at *www.patreon.com/StephaniePaola.*

Dr. Rosie Ramos

Rosie Ramos, Ed.D., MSW is the author of *Teach Me With Cariño: Head Start Teachers' Perspectives of Culturally Responsive Pedagogy in Preschool Classrooms* (2018) and *Compassion is Not Weakness!* (2019/2020). Most recently, Dr. Rosie's article, "A la Fregada con el Chronic STRESS!!!" was published by *Saint Lunita Magazine* (2022) created by Las Doctoras. A Latina feminist of Puerto Rican/Mexican roots, she was born and raised in East Los Angeles. Dr. Rosie proudly produces various educational plays utilizing teatro as a teaching vehicle, to bring social awareness throughout Latino communities from East Los Angeles, CA to New York City. Poetry is a new artistic journey that Dr. Rosie is now embracing and ready to share with Raza!

Sanjuanita (Sanjui) Martinez

Sanjui (Sanjuanita Martinez) is a secondary teacher employed by LAUSD. She has a total of 35 years of teaching experience. She is the mother of four adult children. She enjoys time reading and/or writing short stories and poetry (while enjoying a cup of coffee). She hopes to publish her first collection of poetry in the near future. She has a chihuahua named Oreo who accompanies her every year to Texas to visit family.

Lois Jackson King

A retired educator with degrees in Social Behavior, Christian Education and Christian Counseling as well as an Ordained Minister of the Gospel. Mother of 4, a grandmother of 10, a great-grandmother of 11, and one great-great-granddaughter.

Michelle Smith

A Los Angeles native, a Gemini, a poet, essayist, novice painter, and photographer. The color teal, seashells, roses and sunflowers in a blue glass vase, and water aerobics are a few of my favorite things; however, my autistic son and employment are my life-long and loving journeys.

Alayna Abravanel

Alayna Abravanel joined our Conchas y Café workshop series after participating in our *Journal of My Life* series offered in partnership with the Los Angeles Public Library. Alayna tries to express herself in as many was as she can.

Abraham Jaramillo

Abraham Jaramillo is a multimedia artist; illustrator, graphic designer, and photographer. His love for the arts began back when he created small sketch galleries for his grandmother when he was 8 years old. A longtime volunteer and teaching artist with DSTL Arts, Abraham enjoys and nurtures the pursuit of knowledge both in himself and others.

Royal Roots

Royal Roots is a self taught Afro-Indigenous multimedia artist who uses art to reclaim her cultural heritage and uplift her people. Through poetry, song, dance and art she honors her roots in Mexico and Central America. Her creations are made to remind people of their connection to Mother Earth and each other.

About the Conchas y Café program

Conchas y Café is a 12-week workshop series for adults, focusing exclusively on creative writing, literacy, and illustration. Participants have the opportunity to work with volunteer writers and artists on developing artwork that will be published and presented in a triannual 'zine and public reading.

For more information, locations, and dates for upcoming Conchas y Café workshops, contact us by email at *info@DSTLArts.org*.

Acerca el programa Conchas y Café

Conchas y Café es un taller de 12 semanas para adultos, especializando en escritura, literatura, y dibujo. Participantes tienen la oportunidad de trabajar con escritores y artistas voluntarios en el desarrollo de obras de arte que serán publicados y presentados en publicaciones trimestrales y lecturas públicas.

Para más información, localidades, y fechas de próximos talleres de Conchas y Café, contáctenos por correo electronico al *info@DSTLArts.org*.

This program is supported in part by:

Caring for the World: Conchas y Café Zine; Vol. 7, Issue 2
available now at **DSTLArts.org/shop**

This publication was produced by DSTL Arts.

DSTL Arts is a nonprofit arts mentorship organization that inspires, teaches, and hires emerging artists from underserved communities.

To learn more about DSTL Arts, visit online at:
DSTLArts.org

 @DSTLArts